THE 2025 BRAND TONE & TERMINOLOGY GUIDE FOR AMERICAN INDIE GAME DEVELOPERS LOCALIZING INTO JAPANESE

by Kyle Murphey

INTRODUCTION

Venturing into the Japanese market as an American indie game developer is an invitation to immerse yourself in one of the world's most storied and discerning gaming cultures. Japan's players grew up on legends: Nintendo, Square Enix, Capcom, and many others who set benchmarks for quality, narrative depth, and emotional resonance. To thrive here, you must offer more than a direct translation. You need a holistic localization strategy that respects linguistic nuances, embraces cultural subtleties, and resonates with the values and aesthetics that Japanese players hold dear.

Achieving this involves a careful recalibration of tone, narrative, and presentation. Subtlety, sincerity, and humility often win over the hearts of Japanese gamers, who may feel alienated by overly boastful claims or overly casual, slang-heavy communication. Craftsmanship and emotional storytelling matter deeply. Instead of bombastic self-praise, invite players to discover your world at their own pace. Convey artistry, reliability, and a willingness to learn from their feedback.

This guide lays out a path for transforming your brand voice, selecting culturally aligned terminology, handling humor, formatting text, engaging communities, choosing marketing channels, adapting to seasonal events, fairly pricing content, understanding your competition, refining character dialogue, conducting thorough QA, and sustaining long-term improvements. Each section offers practical examples—translated phrases, adjusted marketing lines, scenario-based suggestions—to help you create a genuinely immersive and respectful experience. By approaching localization as a form of cultural diplomacy, your indie title can transcend borders, evolving into something Japanese players not only accept, but genuinely cherish.

1. UNDERSTANDING THE JAPANESE GAMING LANDSCAPE

The Japanese gaming landscape is a tapestry woven from decades of pioneering titles and beloved characters. Players here are neither easily impressed by surface-level flash nor persuaded by raw hype. Instead, they revere nuanced storytelling, deep emotional arcs, and clear evidence of creative dedication. To connect with this audience, think like a craftsman offering a beautifully carved piece rather than a salesperson pitching the "best deal ever."

In practice, this means shifting from proclamations of "epic" adventures toward promises of heartfelt narratives and meaningful player experiences. Instead of saying "Our game is the greatest!" consider framing your message as: "私たちは、細部まで丁寧に作り込んだ物語をお届けします" ("We deliver a story meticulously crafted down to the finest detail."). This speaks to an appreciation for effort and sincerity rather than ego-driven claims.

Cultural expectations also mean respecting subtlety over aggression. Phrases that work in American marketing—"Don't miss this chance!"—might feel pushy. A gentler "ぜひお楽しみください" ("Please enjoy at your leisure.") recognizes the player's agency and comfort. Japanese gamers often connect more strongly when they sense humility and authenticity. They value quiet confidence, gradual discovery, and the feeling that they are respected participants, not targets. By beginning with an understanding of these landscape traits, you'll lay a solid foundation for all your localization efforts. Each linguistic choice, narrative angle, and user interaction can then build upon this cultural insight, resulting in a more harmonious and compelling presence in one of the world's most revered gaming markets.

Key Cultural Insights:

- **Long-Standing Gaming Tradition:**
  - Japanese gamers expect narrative complexity and smooth gameplay.
  - *Example:* If your American marketing says "Experience the most epic storyline ever!", consider: "壮大で心に響く物語をお届けします" (Sōdai de kokoro ni hibiku monogatari o otodoke shimasu) → "We deliver a grand, heart-touching story." This implies depth and care rather than mere hype.
- **Value on Subtlety and Respect:**
  - Instead of "Don't miss out!" try something gentler and more respectful: "ぜひお楽しみください" (Zehi o-tanoshimi kudasai) → "By all means, please enjoy."
- **Quality and Craftsmanship:**
  - If you'd say "Our indie studio rocks!" consider: "小さなチームですが、職人技のゲーム作りにこだわっています" (Chīsana chīmu desu ga, shokunin-waza no gēmu-zukuri ni kodawatte imasu) → "We are a small team committed to an artisan's approach to game-making."
- **Narrative and Emotional Engagement:**
  - Replace straightforward boasts with an emotional promise: "キャラクターたちの運命に心を揺さぶられる物語をどうぞ" (Kyarakutā-tachi no unmei ni kokoro o yusaburareru monogatari o dōzo) → "Please experience a story that will stir your heart with the fate of its characters."

2. ADAPTING THE BRAND VOICE

Adapting your brand voice involves translating more than words. It's about capturing the right emotional register, level of politeness, and sense of partnership. American indie studios often project familiarity, humor, and informal excitement. While friendly, this approach might feel off-balance in Japan, where polite humility and gentle encouragement resonate more deeply.

Instead of "Hey guys, ready to kick some butt?" consider "皆さま、準備はよろしいでしょうか？新たな冒険が待っています" ("Everyone, are you ready? A new adventure awaits."). Replace slang and cultural in-jokes with more universal appeals, focusing on the shared journey rather than a one-sided boast. Use "です/ます" forms for neutrality and politeness. Show gratitude frequently: "皆さまのご支援に感謝します" ("We appreciate your support") underscores that the player's time and interest are genuinely valued.

Even calls to action require a gentle touch. Instead of "Grab our awesome skins now!" say "新しいスキンで、物語をさらに彩ってみませんか？" ("Why not enhance your story with these new skins?"). This phrasing invites rather than compels. Over time, this measured, respectful tone conveys sincerity and positions your brand as a thoughtful contributor to the gaming dialogue, not an outsider shouting for attention. As you refine your voice, remember that trust is earned gradually. By consistently speaking in a manner that respects local sensibilities, you demonstrate empathy, cultural literacy, and a commitment to providing meaningful value. The end result? Players who feel welcome, not targeted—participants in a shared experience, not just customers.

From American Casual to Japanese Polite-Approachable:

- **Original Tone (English):** "Hey, guys! Get ready to kick some serious butt in our awesome new update!"
- **Adapted Tone (Japanese):** "皆さま、こんにちは。新アップデートで、さらなる挑戦が待っています。ぜひお試しください。" (Minasama, konnichiwa. Shin appudēto de, saranaru chōsen ga matte imasu. Zehi o-tameshi kudasai.) → "Hello, everyone. A new challenge awaits in our latest update. Please give it a try."

Do's and Don'ts:

- **Do:**
  - Use "です/ます" forms, e.g., "楽しめます" (tanoshimemasu, you can enjoy), "お届けします" (otodoke shimasu, we deliver).
  - Show gratitude, e.g., "皆さまのサポートに感謝しています" (Minasama no sapōto ni kansha shite imasu) → "We appreciate everyone's support."
- **Don't:**
  - Overuse slang or imperatives: "Don't miss out!" → "お見逃しなく" (o-misogashinaku) is acceptable, but try to keep a softer tone.
  - Rely on humor that references American TV, slang like "awesome sauce," or phrases like "killin' it!"

More Examples:

- "Level up and dominate!" → "キャラクターを成長させ、新たな力を試してみましょう。" (Kyarakutā o seichō sasete, aratana chikara o tameshite mimashō.) → "Grow your character and test your newfound strength."
- "You'll love our brand-new skins!" → "新しいスキンで、冒険をより華やかに彩ってみませんか？" (Atarashii sukin de, bōken o yori hanayaka ni irodotte mimasen ka?) → "Why not add extra flair to your adventure with our new skins?"

3. TERMINOLOGY AND KEYWORDS

Your choice of words influences how players perceive your world. In Japanese localization, familiar gaming loanwords like "クエスト" (quest) and "ダンジョン" (dungeon) ease comprehension, while carefully chosen native terms highlight artisanal quality or narrative significance. Selecting culturally resonant vocabulary grounds your game in language that feels authentic, not forced.

For example, conveying the idea of a handcrafted experience might shift from "handmade" to "丁寧に作り込まれた" (carefully crafted), which implies dedication and craftsmanship. If your game is about building trust and community, words like "仲間" (nakama, companions) carry a warm, inclusive tone—more heartfelt than a simple "party members."

Cultural fit matters, too. Aggressive terms like "dominate" or "conquer" might feel out of place. Instead, consider "挑戦する" (chōsen suru, to challenge) or "冒険する" (bōken suru, to go adventuring). Such vocabulary presents heroic deeds as journeys rather than violent boasts. Even item names can be reimagined. A "Mega Healing Potion" becomes "極上回復薬" (gokujō kaifukuyaku, finest healing medicine), hinting at rarity and quality rather than raw size.

Building a consistent lexicon ensures coherence across your UI, dialogue, marketing materials, and patch notes. Maintain a glossary of terms—adventurer, guild, epic, magic—and decide on their Japanese counterparts in advance. By doing so, you prevent tonal drift and reinforce a clear, culturally tuned identity.

Ultimately, thoughtful terminology is the linguistic framework that lets Japanese players immediately understand your world's logic, values, and atmosphere, strengthening immersion and long-term engagement.

Game-Related Terms:

- "Adventurer" → "冒険者" (bōkensha)
- "Hero" → "勇者" (yūsha) for a fantasy setting, "主人公" (shujinkō) if more narrative-focused
- "Magic" → "魔法" (mahō)
- "Guild" → "ギルド" (girudo), a direct loanword commonly used
- "Update" → "アップデート" (appudēto), or "更新" (kōshin) if you prefer a native Japanese term for "renewal/update"

Brand Value Expressions:

- "Handcrafted" → "手作り" (tezukuri) or "丁寧に作り込まれた" (teinei ni tsukurikomareta, carefully crafted)
- "Indie Developer" → "インディー開発者" (indī kaihatsusha) or "小規模スタジオ" (shōkibo sutajio, small-scale studio)
- "Sustainable, Ethical Approach" → "持続可能な制作姿勢" (jizoku kanō na seisaku shisei)

Cultural Sensitivity in Word Choice:

- Instead of "epic loot," consider:
  - "貴重なアイテム" (kichō na aitemu, valuable items)
  - "特別な宝物" (tokubetsu na takaramono, special treasures)

4. CULTURAL REFERENCES, HUMOR, AND NARRATIVE ELEMENTS

Cultural references and humor can unite audiences—or alienate them if mishandled. Jokes rooted in American pop culture or sports metaphors may confuse Japanese players. Aim for humor that transcends borders. A shy monster that accidentally showers foes with flower petals instead of fireballs can amuse universally, while a line referencing U.S. late-night TV might fall flat.

Your narrative elements should also reflect themes that resonate broadly. Emotional depth, moral dilemmas, and quiet moments of character growth play well in Japan. Instead of relying on slapstick or pop-culture zingers, cultivate gentle wit and endearing quirks. For example, an NPC might say "魔法を間違えちゃったみたいで、火球の代わりに花びらが舞っちゃいました" ("It seems I messed up my spell, and instead of a fireball, petals danced through the air"). This scenario is charming without relying on references that don't travel well.

If your original script leans on jokes about American celebrities or holidays, replace them with either universal topics—like the joy of discovering a rare item—or subtle cultural homages that feel natural to your game's setting. Remember that subtlety often outshines brash humor. Understatement and gentle irony frequently appeal to Japanese sensibilities, so consider adding depth through subtext rather than punchlines. By crafting narrative elements with careful cultural consideration, you encourage players to engage with your story at a level that feels welcoming, intriguing, and truly theirs to explore.

Cultural Adaptation of Content:

- American Reference: "Ready to tackle this challenge like an NFL player?" → Confusing for many Japanese players.
- Instead: "新たな戦いに心の準備はできていますか？" (Aratana tatakai ni kokoro no junbi wa dekite imasu ka?) → "Are you ready at heart for the new battles ahead?"

Emotional and Narrative Depth:

- A joke about a late-night taco stand might miss the mark. Instead, show humor through a character's bashful apology or an NPC's quirky hobby.
- For example, a wizard who mixes up spells: "おや？火球を出すつもりが、花びらを飛ばしてしまいました。" (Oya? Kakyū o dasu tsumori ga, hanabira o tobashite shimaimashita.) → "Oh dear, I meant to cast a fireball, but ended up scattering flower petals instead."

5. FORMATTING, CONVENTIONS & VISUAL ELEMENTS

Precise formatting and visual clarity are silent ambassadors of respect. Japanese text conventions differ from English: dates follow the YYYY年MM月DD日 format, measurements favor the metric system, and currency is displayed in yen without decimals. Beyond these basics, consider how text spacing, line breaks, and font choices can affect readability.

For instance, Japanese doesn't require spaces between words. Proper line breaks, balanced white space, and well-chosen fonts ensure players never struggle to parse your text. A crowded UI or overly long item descriptions might exhaust the reader. Instead, aim for brevity and clarity in tooltips, avoiding run-on sentences.

Visual elements also matter. Symbols, icons, and layout should align with local expectations. For example, a scroll icon might be less intuitive than a simple arrow or a Japanese label indicating "次へ" ("next"). Maintaining consistency in iconography, color coding, and menu structure helps players feel immediately at home.

Even subtle details—like ensuring that tutorial pop-ups are properly centered, or that the text doesn't overlap character portraits—convey professionalism and care. These choices assure players that you're not just translating text, but refining the entire experience for their comfort. Ultimately, mindful formatting and polished visuals create an environment where your story and gameplay mechanics shine, unobstructed by awkward presentation or linguistic confusion.

Writing Conventions & UI Examples:

- Date: "2024年12月20日" instead of "December 20, 2024"
- Currency: Use "円" without decimals, e.g., "1,200円" not "¥1,200.00"
- Menu example: Instead of "START GAME," use "ゲーム開始" (Gēmu kaishi).
- Keep descriptive item/tooltips concise and direct. Avoid multiple lines of very long sentences.

Legibility and Aesthetics:

- Choose a font that displays kana and kanji clearly.
- Ensure text spacing: Japanese doesn't use spaces between words, so line breaks and font choice are critical to readability.

6. COMMUNITY ENGAGEMENT AND CUSTOMER SUPPORT

Building a lasting relationship with Japanese players means listening intently and responding with thoughtfulness. Community engagement isn't just about announcing patches—it's about acknowledging feedback, celebrating player contributions, and treating criticism as an opportunity to improve. A polite, measured tone in forums, social media, and Q&A sessions indicates respect and attentiveness.

When players express concerns, a reply like "貴重なご意見ありがとうございます。改善を検討いたします" ("Thank you for your valuable feedback. We'll consider improvements") can strengthen goodwill. Following through on these promises—adding requested quality-of-life changes or clarifying confusing mechanics—demonstrates that you genuinely value their input. Over time, this dialogue fosters trust, encouraging players to stay with your game longer and invest more emotionally.

Consider hosting periodic community surveys, dev diaries, or even in-game events celebrating player creativity. A small shout-out in patch notes—"プレイヤーの皆さまから頂いたアイデアをもとに、新スキンを追加しました" ("Based on your ideas, we've added a new skin")—builds a sense of shared ownership. In Japanese culture, humility and gratitude are appreciated virtues. When you approach customer support as a partnership rather than a necessary chore, players feel that you're crafting the experience together. The end result is a community that not only supports your game, but becomes an active participant in its ongoing evolution.

Community Communication Examples:

- "Thank you for your feedback" → "貴重なご意見をありがとうございます" (Kichōna go-iken o arigatō gozaimasu)
- "We are working on improvements" → "改善に向けて努力しています" (Kaizen ni mukete doryoku shite imasu)

Long-Term Engagement:

- Consider posting patch notes in Japanese with a polite preface and a closing note of thanks.
- Host Q&A sessions where you acknowledge player questions: "皆さまのご質問にお答えします" (Minasama no go-shitsumon ni o-kotae shimasu) → "We will answer everyone's questions."

7. MARKETING CHANNELS AND PROMOTIONAL STRATEGY

Japan's digital ecosystem revolves around specific platforms, influencer cultures, and communication styles. Understanding where and how to present your game is crucial. Twitter (X), YouTube, and streaming communities like NicoNico Douga are popular channels. Rather than loud advertising, consider partnering with a respected gaming influencer who can authentically present your title.

For example, coordinate with a Japanese VTuber who enjoys indie games. Provide them with a well-prepared press kit in Japanese—clear summary, key features, story hints—and allow them to share your game naturally with their audience. The influencer's personal connection with their fans lends credibility, and their measured enthusiasm can resonate more than a hard-sell pitch.

Keep your marketing language consistent with your brand voice. A tweet announcing a new update might say: "【新情報】本日、新アップデートをリリースしました。ぜひ新たな冒険をお楽しみください" ("[New Info] We've released a new update today. Please enjoy the new adventure."). This tone is inviting, informative, and devoid of aggressive salesmanship.

Paid ads can still play a role, but consider cultural norms when crafting their text. Subtle, respectful messaging often converts better than flashy calls to action. Over time, as your game gains traction, you can leverage player testimonials and user-generated content. Showcasing positive community reactions tells prospective players that your title has earned a place in local hearts—a far more compelling narrative than any tagline you could invent yourself.

Popular Channels & Collaborations:

- Twitter announcement example: "【新情報】アップデート配信開始しました！ぜひ新たな冒険をお楽しみください。" (Shinjōhō: appudēto haishin kaishi shimashita! Zehi aratana bōken o o-tanoshimi kudasai.) → "[New Info] The update is now live! Please enjoy the new adventure."
- Working with a known Japanese indie reviewer: Provide them with review keys and a clear, respectful press kit in Japanese.

Strategic Positioning:

- Highlight the uniqueness: "独特な世界観で描かれた物語" (Dokutokuna sekaikan de egakareta monogatari) → "A story painted with a unique worldview."

8. SEASONAL AND HOLIDAY ADAPTATIONS

Tapping into Japan's seasonal rhythms and cultural events can endear your game to local players. Cherry blossom (桜, sakura) season in spring, summer festivals, autumn foliage viewing, and New Year's celebrations offer natural opportunities for themed content. Players will appreciate events that reflect their own traditions—like a special "お正月イベント" (New Year's event) offering auspicious in-game items.

Think about introducing limited-time quests tied to cultural motifs. In spring, you might present a sakura-themed questline that rewards a "桜色のマント" (cherry blossom-colored cape). During summer festival season, consider "お祭り" decorations or fireworks-inspired challenges. A subtle narrative hook—an NPC reminiscing about a yearly harvest festival—invites players to celebrate these moments with you.

Keep these adaptations tasteful and relevant to your game's world. If your setting is fantasy, align seasonal elements with that theme. For example, during Tanabata (a star festival), you might offer a constellation-themed armor set or a quest to gather "星屑" (stardust). Such gestures show that you respect local cultural touchstones and are making genuine efforts to engage with the calendar that Japanese players know and love.

By integrating these seasonal elements, you transform your game from a static product into a living experience that acknowledges players' cultural lives. This responsiveness strengthens bonds, creating a sense of place and time that resonates powerfully within the Japanese gaming community.

Event Localization Examples:

- Cherry Blossom (Spring): Offer a "桜色の衣装" (Sakurairo no isshō, cherry blossom-colored costume) during spring.
- New Year's: Include a "お正月特別クエスト" (Oshōgatsu tokubetsu kuesuto, special New Year's quest) with auspicious items like "縁起物" (engimono, lucky charms).

9. PRICING, MONETIZATION, AND CUSTOMER PERCEPTION

Fair, transparent pricing and considerate monetization strategies reinforce trust. Japanese players value quality over quantity and prefer not to feel coerced. Present premium content as an enhancement, not a necessity. Explain that new DLC offers "より深い物語体験" ("an even deeper narrative experience") rather than just pushing limited-time deals.

Set reasonable, locally considerate price points—adjusting to yen and market norms. If you offer microtransactions, emphasize that they're optional treats. For example, "新しいスキンはお好みでお選びいただけます" ("You may choose the new skins if you like") suggests freedom rather than pressure. Avoid phrases like "don't miss out," which can sound intrusive; instead, try "ご興味があれば、お試しください" ("If you're interested, please give it a try").

Regularly communicate how revenue supports continued development or better servers. Framing paid content as a mutual investment—players support the studio, and the studio delivers higher quality—can feel more equitable. If players sense you're prioritizing their experience over profit, they become more open to occasional purchases.

Over time, fair pricing and honest communication establish your reputation. Players share positive experiences with friends, confident that your studio respects their gaming ecosystem and won't exploit their love for the game. This loyalty cannot be bought—it must be earned through consistent transparency and value.

Fair and Transparent Pricing Examples:

- "This DLC costs $5.99!" → Convert pricing thoughtfully, e.g., "600円" (balanced for local value).
- Instead of "Limited time only, buy now!" say: "期間限定の特別コンテンツをご用意しました。ぜひご検討ください。" (Kikan gentei no tokubetsu kontentsu o go-yōi shimashita. Zehi go-kentō kudasai.) → "We've prepared special, limited-time content. Please consider it at your leisure."

10. COMPETITOR CONTEXT AND INSPIRATION

You're entering a landscape where titans like Nintendo, Capcom, and Bandai Namco have set high standards. Observing their approach can teach you what resonates with Japanese players. Note how these studios communicate updates: calmly, clearly, and with a sense of gratitude. Their trailers often highlight story, character, and artistry rather than boasting.

This doesn't mean you must mimic them. Instead, find your unique identity and present it with the same respect and care. If your game emphasizes a heartfelt narrative, convey that rather than forcing epic claims. Consider a phrase like "新たな世界で紡がれる静かで深い物語" ("A quiet, deep story woven in a new world") to hint at depth and authenticity.

Study how beloved series adapt over time. They often engage fans by balancing tradition and innovation—adding new features while honoring what players already love. Emulate this respect for audience expectations. If a known RPG series celebrates its legacy in press releases or developer notes, you can highlight how your indie title shares certain values: dedication to player satisfaction, narrative richness, or careful craft.

In this way, even as a newcomer, you demonstrate your understanding of cultural and industry norms. Rather than positioning yourself as a challenger shouting for attention, you show that you've studied the local language—both literally and metaphorically—and are committed to contributing something meaningful to the tapestry of Japanese gaming culture.

Learning from Domestic Titles:

- Study "Nintendo Direct" presentations: They are calm, direct, and informative rather than hyperbolic.
- Notice how titles like "Dragon Quest" emphasize tradition, legacy, and a beloved continuity.

Carving Your Niche:

- "我々の作品は、懐かしさと新鮮さを融合させた独自の冒険です。" (Wareware no sakuhin wa, natsukashisa to shinshensa o yūgō saseta dokuji no bōken desu.) → "Our work is a unique adventure that blends nostalgia with freshness."

11. VOICEOVER, NAMING CONVENTIONS & CHARACTER DIALOGUE

Voiceover and naming choices profoundly influence atmosphere. Japanese voice actors bring authenticity and emotional nuance. Selecting a known voice actor or ensuring your lines match the character's personality and social status enhances credibility. A wise mentor might speak more formally, while a mischievous rogue adopts a lighter, casual tone—still polite enough, but playful.

Naming conventions matter. Complex, unpronounceable names alienate players. If your English script has "Thyreldown the Unending," consider a phonetic approximation that flows in Japanese: "サイレドウン" (Sairedoun). Alternatively, choose simpler names that evoke mood without confusing syllables. Consistency also counts: if you use kanji for certain factions, apply the same logic to similar groups.

In dialogue, avoid overly direct American humor. Let a character's traits shine through subtle interactions. A shopkeeper might say: "今日も珍しい品が入荷しましたよ" ("We've got some rare items in stock today"), casually inviting curiosity. Over time, these speech patterns shape player perception of your world's social fabric.

When casting voice actors, brief them on character backgrounds and emotional beats. Authentic line delivery can be the difference between a character feeling flat or alive. By mastering voice and name conventions, you invite Japanese players into a world where every character, place, and object aligns with their linguistic expectations—deepening immersion and emotional connection.

Voice Acting & Character Dialogue Examples:

- A mentor character might speak softly and respectfully: "あなたの成長を見守っています。" (Anata no seichō o mimamotte imasu.) → "I am watching over your growth."
- A playful shopkeeper NPC: "いらっしゃいませ！今日も珍しいアイテムが入荷しましたよ。" (Irasshaimase! Kyō mo mezurashii aitemu ga nyūka shimashita yo.) → "Welcome! We've stocked some rare items again today."

Item & Menu Naming:

- Instead of "Mega Ultra Healing Potion," try "極上回復薬" (gokujō kaifukuyaku) → "Finest Healing Medicine."
- Keep naming conventions consistent with your game's setting—if it's fantasy, choose slightly archaic terms; if sci-fi, opt for sharper, modern-sounding loanwords.

12. QUALITY ASSURANCE IN LOCALIZATION

Quality assurance (QA) isn't just proofreading. It's a holistic process ensuring your Japanese localization feels natural, consistent, and respectful. Engage professional translators familiar with gaming terminology, and have native-speaking testers play through the title, scanning for awkward phrasing, culturally jarring jokes, or unclear instructions.

Encourage testers to note any confusion: does an NPC's dialogue sound too casual or too formal? Are tutorial instructions too long-winded? Are item descriptions too vague? Adjust accordingly. Even minor changes—fixing a strange line break, rewording a boss introduction—show that you care about the player's comfort and immersion.

After initial fixes, run a second testing round. If players report that a certain pun still falls flat or a particular side quest's lore is murky, refine again. This iterative approach mirrors the craftsmanship Japanese players admire. Rather than rushing, you're carving your narrative and language into a more precise, elegant form.

In doing so, you distinguish yourself from competitors who settle for basic translation. Your attention to detail becomes evident as players sense the game was fine-tuned just for them. This thorough QA transforms localization into a living art form, aligning perfectly with Japan's appreciation for careful, attentive refinement.

Review Process & User Testing:

- Provide testers with context for each line. Ask if the tone feels right, if the humor makes sense, and if instructions are clear.
- After adjustments, re-test to confirm improvements.

13. LONG-TERM EVOLUTION AND UPDATES

Localization isn't static; it's an ongoing dialogue. As your Japanese audience grows, they'll share opinions about story pacing, difficulty balance, or even UI elements. Listen, adapt, and communicate changes back in a manner that respects their input. Over time, these refinements become part of your brand's character—an evolving work of art shaped by a community's voice.

If players suggest more lore or request subtler hints in puzzles, respond by integrating small narrative additions. Announce improvements thoughtfully: "皆さまの声に応え、NPCの会話に新たな背景要素を加えました" ("Responding to your feedback, we've added new background elements to NPC dialogue."). Such updates show you're attentive, reinforcing trust and goodwill.

Seasons, technology, and cultural trends evolve. Remain curious and flexible. If streaming culture grows, integrate Twitch or YouTube gaming events with Japanese subtitles. If certain storytelling themes trend—like environmental stewardship—consider weaving subtle references into your narratives. Consistent growth ensures your title remains relevant and beloved.

Eventually, players come to see you not as a foreign developer, but as a friend who understands their gaming language, both literally and figuratively. This bonds them to your brand and encourages them to support future projects. Through continuous attention, you transform localization from a launch-day task into a long-term cultural exchange.

Continuous Refinement & Brand Loyalty:

- If players request more lore in the NPC dialogue, add subtle narrative hints in future patches.
- Announce changes: "皆さまの声をもとに、NPCの会話をより深くしました。" (Minasama no koe o moto ni, NPC no kaiwa o yori fukaku shimashita.) → "Based on your feedback, we've deepened the NPC conversations."

CONCLUSION

By embracing these cultural, linguistic, and aesthetic insights, you transform your localized game into a product that feels native to the Japanese landscape. This journey demands patience, research, and empathy—qualities that, once cultivated, open doors to genuine cross-cultural connection. Rather than appearing as an outsider forcing foreign concepts, you present yourself as a respectful guest, eager to learn and share.

Localization is more than finding equivalent words. It's about understanding the values behind those words, the emotional weight they carry, and the expectations that shape how players perceive them. Each carefully chosen phrase, respectfully written patch note, and culturally attuned event weaves a narrative of sincerity and craftsmanship. The payoff is a vibrant, engaged community of players who feel seen and appreciated.

Over time, as your updates continue, your community grows, and your understanding deepens, the line between "foreign" and "local" blurs. Your game stands on equal footing with domestic titles, acknowledged for its quality, narrative richness, and respectful treatment of players. This fusion of cultures becomes its own form of art, proving that great stories transcend borders when told with understanding, humility, and genuine passion.

KYLE MURPHEY

KYLE MURPHEY

KYLE MURPHEY

KYLE MURPHEY

THE 2025 BRAND TONE & TERMINOLOGY GUIDE FOR AMERICAN INDIE GAM...

KYLE MURPHEY

www.ingramcontent.com/pod-product-compliance
Lightning Source LLC
Chambersburg PA
CBHW070955220526
45471CB00007B/3038